Written by
Sylva Nnaekpe

Copyright © 2020 Sylva Nnaekpe.

All rights reserved. No part of this book can be reproduced by any Medium, graphic, electronic or mechanical, including photocopies, recording or by any system of storage and recovery of information without the permission for written from the editor except in the case of short quotes in critical articles and reviews.

You can make book orders from Silsnorra Publishing
and in bookstores

Due to the dynamic nature of the internet, any web address or Link content in this book may have changed since its post And it may no longer be valid. The Opinions expressed in this work are Exclusively from the author and do
not necessarily reflect the opinions of the editor
Who, by this means, renounces any responsibility about them.

ISBN: 978-1-951792-78-7(Soft Cover)
ISBN: 978-1-951792-79-4 (Hard Cover)
ISBN 978-1-951792-80-0 (electronic book)
ISBN 978-1-951792-81-7 (Notebook)

Printing information available on the last page.
Silsnorra Publishing Review Date: 01/18/2020

Once upon a time on a beautiful Saturday morning, Ivry's friends came over to her house to spend time with her in preparation for her big day. Ivry was about to turn six, and her parents planned a costume party for her. Ivry and her friends sat in her room and brainstormed what costumes to wear to celebrate her birthday. The kids were so excited as they scanned through the pages of the costume catalog to find an outfit.

"I will be a fairy. Fairies are kind, they
have magical powers,
love sparkles, use a magic wand
to make things bloom, and love
plants too," Ivry said.

"The princess costume is beautiful. I will be a princess on your big day Ivry. A Princess is brave, compassionate, strong, confident, pampered, and kind," said Tini.

"Be a superhero on your big day Ivry. Superheroes have extraordinary powers. They are courageous, have a great sense of responsibility, know how to fight, defend others, and save the world," Ivry said to herself with a smile, her eyes blazing like the stars.

"I, Jose will be a chef on Ivry's big day. A chef can cook, pay attention to details, is creative, and work well in a team," Jose said with a smile and continued,

"Ivry,

I think you should dress like a medical professional, a doctor, a nurse, a scientist, or a caregiver. Medical professionals have excellent communication skills; they are compassionate, active, can multitask, and take good care of the sick."

"Look! This costume reminds me of my uncle Tom, who is an engineer. Engineers think logically, are team players, problem solves, construct beautiful things, and pay attention to details," said Tini

"It is so fun to hear us discuss, share our opinions, and gain insight into what the costumes represent. I think one of us should dress like a granny. Nana's and Papas are too cute. They always have cookies, love unconditionally, know everything, understand everything, and are good listeners.

I always look forward to every other weekend spent with my nana and papa because it is ever memorable and fun. Grannies are just like teachers; dedicated, committed, brilliant, care, and engage me in learning," said Ivry.

"How about Kiki dress like a farmer? Farmers do a great job producing a variety of foods; people need them every day.

Farmers are patient; they work hard, cultivate our food, and take a significant risk all year round," said Jose.

"Look! The mailman's costume." Jose pointed to the catalog. "It's beautiful," echoed his friends. The mailman interacts with the public, is cautious, well detailed when it comes to sorting our mails, performs his job correctly, and make sure our letters, packages, and bills get to our parents on time," Jose said.

"Ivry, I wonder what you would look like dressed as a police officer on your big day. Police officers uphold order, protect people, and property. They also control traffic, respond to emergencies, and patrol neighborhoods to ensure everyone is safe." said Tini.

Little Ivry and her friends
were so focused on their discussion,
and laughter as they brainstormed on
what costumes to wear for
her big day and did not notice
Ivry's mum walked into her room.

She listened to Ivry, and her friends discuss for some minutes and then interrupted their conversation. " Hello - hello- hello, beautiful people. You have been in your room all day. You missed lunch and completely forgot it was time for dinner. Is everything alright?" She asked.

"Yes, mum, everything is fine. My friends and I went through the catalog to pick out what costume to wear in celebration of my birthday. We found many outfits that made it hard for us to make a choice. Do you have any unique ideas, mum?" Ivry asked.

"Costumes and uniforms come with lots of responsibilities and tasks.

I think you all should be whatever you want that makes you happy, especially as you celebrate with friends and family on your special day.

Birthday celebrations are beautiful. It is also another way of showing loved ones how much you cherish them, and care.

What truly matters in all this is that in whatever you choose to be, do it with gratitude and a thankful heart.

Remember, you all are welcome to be whatever you choose that makes you truly happy as you celebrate your friend's' big day." Ivry's mum said to Ivry and her friends. She gave them a hug and left the room.

Ivry's big day finally came.

Ivry, Tini, Jose, and their friends looked as beautiful as ever, in their chosen attire.

www.ingramcontent.com/pod-product-compliance
Lightning Source LLC
Chambersburg PA
CBHW081759100526
44592CB00015B/2492